Edge and Fold

Edge and Fold

—

Two Poems by Paul Hoover

Apogee Press
Berkeley · California
2006

For Maxine, Koren, Philip, and Julian

Edge and Fold I-X were published in *Transfer* (editors: Aaron "Green" LaFleur and Lauren Quinn). They also appeared online in *Jacket* (guest editor: Pam Brown).

Edge and Fold XI-XX were published in the chapbook series *Both Both* (editor: John Sakkis).

Edge and Fold XVI-XIX were published in *The New Review of Literature* (poetry editor: Dennis Phillips).

Edge and Fold XXXI-XXXV were published in *Square One* (editors: Casady Monroe, Patrick Kelling, and Jennifer Dunbar Dorn).

Edge and Fold XXXVI-XL were published in *Five Fingers Review* (editor: Jaime Robles).

Edge and Fold XLIX was published on the *Conjunctions* website in memory of Robert Creeley.

"The Reading" is published here for the first time.

Book design by Philip Krayna Design, Berkeley, California.

©2006 by Paul Hoover.

Cover image: *Ball on Water (Pelota en agua)*, 1994, Gabriel Orozco. Courtesy of the Solomon R. Guggenheim Museum, New York

ISBN 0-9744687-2-x. Library of Congress Control Number 2006927511.

Published by Apogee Press, Post Office Box 8177, Berkeley CA, 94707-8177.

www.apogeepress.com

Contents

Edge and Fold

"Love lasts a world."
—Robin Blaser

I

even in their objects
      the sound of the white ones

flowing through our robes
      great seekers of nothing

among triangulations
      each place has its windows

sagebrush blue
      and not the last stupor

intensity and its likeness
      in love's first lair

II

pageantry answers:
    it simply means distance

but others see appearance
    nodding at its fires

where eaves meet the street
    these are at the table

sound within music
    the structures of water

singing *which each*
    in pornographic proof

III

so little is profound
     even death's clothing

piling up toward
     the ceiling

unspeakable distance
     a grammar of folds

divide me by my oaths
     in a kingdom of scolds

where the rock simply *is*
     and history takes shape

beneath its own tree
     burdened with stones—

violence and her daughters
     love and her boy

IV

rock and drill
  are a single street's remains

where wind blows north
  and the rivers flow south

houses and their kindling
  overlook the sea

the beaches are empty
  and also the fish

excitement's appetite
  is briefer than a pinch

and the cold wind steady

V

here in the future
      the absence of a thing

constrained by its presence
      is considered almost sacred

its new leaves swirling
      old notes gone

the last skin left
      is finally what you are

digression's too far from fate
      and what am I saying

Alles im Wunderland
      or Petra Van Kant's

was the experience
      worth the candle?

VI

a melancholy lyric
    intimate yet distant

its brokenness is real
    even in the healing

so beauty is halfness
    its truest note cracked

Miles Davis unfulfilled
    his notes heartbreakingly

always on the edge
    of breaking down completely

all true things are song
    a weave unweaving

VII

life tries to keep you
      how far have we come

products of a thinking
      expressions of snow

we taste the river
      often in our drowning

sacred to the world
      of which we are (a)part

Zeno's arrow
      reaches its horizon

stopping as it goes
      the snow that never falls

melts on your face—
      obscurities of the page

and certainties
      at the windows

VIII

edge and fold
      the raiment of the field

the harrow breaks it down
      harrow of sight

with its articulations
      nothing is in passion

when all is in belief
      the world keeps turning

to face the burning sun

IX

the transparent seed
    enters its soil

resident of the world
    for a moment almost nothing

centrifugal but inward
    drawing toward its source

companions and strangers
    the music we are of

X

bright essential speech
    of all things small

and of the last song
    I saved first the twilight

and then a fist of fire
    dwellers of the town

are kneeling on concrete
    in the pleasure of our time

leisure coming after
    I could not defend us

from what we could not be
    crepuscule for tea leaves

the filthy generations
    weakened by a war

XI

he loved the mechanisms
    of wire and device

tipsy monuments
    gadgets of craft

and this of all things
    the most uncertain

an effortless pursuit
    of everything he knows

along the coast of meaning
    where structure is momentum

and life tries to keep him
    in the tuning of a sequence

XII

among the burning questions
    nothing is consumed

the objects are empty
    except for their names

mimetic incarnation
    & shapes of the flowers

"infinite perspectives"
    of a book on architecture

its mind intent on god
    stenographers in an office

transcribing empty space

XIII

the sound is in the wood
    writing its disturbance

as deeply as it can
    this is called music

chromatic and harmonic
    Brahms in the dark

drowning and surviving
    geometric movements

propelled by feeling
    the closer to perception

the more abstract it is
    a cloud of unknowing

crosses all my minds
    what reason for knocking

at an empty house
    what reason for staying

XIV

in a frame of the window
    the branch intervenes

differently each season
    the mind is glass

transparent and painted
    perhaps the still image

thinks to exist
    because we have the time

to seek it and to ask
    the world occurs

its contortions on camera—
    as damage is to glass

several fatal signs
    arrive at present tense

& I refuse perception

XV

the real that's in the world
    is a word intending

absenting all it knows
    a single leaf keeps falling

at the center of an eye
    where the god is hidden

by the brightness it projects
    we have not the strength

to divide ourselves by one
    because it can't speak

the field is now a world
    aimed at attention

XVI

what you don't know
　　doesn't enter in

the paragraph is a mutt
　　and the comma goes away

reality's proposition
　　is problematic, no?

gentlemen, start cognition
　　conception is a whole

she knew about peaches
　　she would make decisions

a curtain if there is one
　　all deep things are song

XVII

world enough and time
    the tough

light of day espousing
    carelessly

the chances we are in
    infinity

has no measure at least
    for several

miles and uncertainty
    is now

the chief source of pleasure
    what can

I tell you when the moon
    goes down

the world's as real
    as thinking

and grasses whip
    the ground

XVIII

in the midst of things
    a winter installation

tracks going back and
    the river in season

though of course diminished
    nothing comes last

there's always one more
    welcome in its passing

as long as there's a rhythm
    the mind's both ways

seeing and reeling
    stealing attention

XIX

think well of distance
    and also Gertrude Stein

mother of the numbers
    what we call fictions

might be alibis
    the thing itself grotesque

in other words average
    without the misshapen

the world would never glow
    our crimes are in the planning

oblique is too direct it's
    out of love we grow

XX

seeing far in the movies
       means you're soon to die

or living as a ghost
       Bruno Ganz for instance

in *Wings of Desire*
       statues and angels

slowly turn their faces
       the utter realism

of a cabbage in your hand
       the uninformed life

is the only one worth living
       in death you reach desire

XXI

lake bed quiet
    covered with snow

windows shining orange
    because of certain dusts

invisible to the eye
    even the road is silent

not a single tire moving
    along with its cold

XXII

exhaling the century's
  left-over smoke

man is but a reed
  in the evenings we can hear

the dampness rolling in
  we're down to the real

& the stations are too far
  a parrot wipes its beak

the universe knows nothing
  crumble of a star

XXIII

attention is a matter
>of supervising shadows

all is arranged for the sake
>of our gardens

there's a final logic
>in everything that is

among such precisions
>a blur is reassuring

at the edge of nature
>a fold creates something

no statue or palace
>at the center of the woods

XXIV

the world is built on sound
    its larks are spreading

even on the night shift
    & silence has no choice

something in the owl
    is coming into its own

in the dark museum
    people crowd into a room

where a video is playing
    light with something in it

XXV

radical weather
    & radical ellipsis

radical patience
    & silence as it is

the surface tension
    of staring too long

the way straight through
    is now the way around

a temporary fix
    for the last

immutable form
    do you whistle

or sing in a style
    that wavers

XXVI

no word
or world

is empty
its horizon's

on the right
& order's

on the run
among inhuman

traffic the
one that's

top gun
we always

love more
the half-complete

man rushing
toward extinction—

well-spoken is
half-sung

XXVII

I shall
say again

what I never
said before

everyone starts
at zero and

some are
at one

love's figured
musicircus

stands sideways
in the aisle

where you can
always see

what you never
saw before

XXVIII

(After Hölderlin)

a series that leads to pain
    also leads to pleasure

one over infinity
    infinity over one

one can only pity
    the gods in their rooms

eyes fixed on the floor
    how lonely it must be

confined to heaven
    your clothes in tatters

the fashions always changing
    it's everything or nothing

and no one comes to call
    except a tender neighbor

who sings your body lightly
    at the end of her senses

XXIX

no room for being
      among the furtive words

being's on its own
      a madman in any language

the sky's a Cadillac
      the head's a cup of tea

what words do we wear
      in earthlight or in shadow

silent fabulations
      softest of gardens

absence is not nothing
      song beyond the singing

XXX

what realism wears
    most inward of fashions

a man walking by water
    is two of us now

digression is closer to truth
    than it is to fate

and dreams are violations
    no privacy at night

everything a symbol
    Empedocles at the brink

tenderly walking back
    to the house where he was born

laurel leaves scratching
    the softest of walls

XXXI

the body is a field
    consisting of attention

singing of a land
    the eye can't imagine

darkness everywhere
    even on the pillow

these are refractions
    of other surface worlds

thickness of a hand
    behind a glass of water

decisions lightning makes
    arriving at the templum

XXXII

mountain moving day
flashbulbs firing

the cloud of unknowing
velocity of water

the earth is other minds
but the speed of a window

is how we change seeing
to be outbound

on the inbound train
among the fierce women

this is the fictive
a latent celebration

of what could never be
a shadow in the rock

exceeds the sun itself
sun exceeds the mind

XXXIII

the first estate is time
    the second is matter

the third estate is shape
    the fourth is shadow

the fifth estate is nothing
    nothing at all

vacant interrogation
    of silence by sound

perception empties
    a room at a time

when the not-yet
    is no longer

and the future
    is unwritten

we know the words it uses
    if not its perfect cadence

XXXIV

when you add to infinity
    the number one

it is and you are
    finite as before

no such thing
    as an infinite measure

the length of life is god
    to stumble on the run

folding and unfolding
    a new blank map

first in the actual
    then as a symbol

XXXV

in the sparest of ruins
    language is act

where one can imagine
    the unbuttoned present

with its ripe interjections
    and swerving cars

the way green mold
    covers a lemon

& stone asks a question
    the moon must answer

XXXVI

impossible leaflets
     are dropped from a plane

and now the town scatters
     beneath information

clutter at the crossing
     every eye dark

from all it doesn't see
     attention alters being

and being disappears
     what a town

and who named it
     every object poses—

chair and its shadow—
     as what they only are

XXXVII

moths on a screen door
    open like mouths

a nearly terminal world
    and comedy in the evening

make tragedy's day complete
    indeterminate meanings

are printed to the ear
    for the mind in question—

as heat withdraws
    from snow

something like euphoria
    relaxes into genius

XXXVIII

fire makes no random assertions
    its fading architecture

exceeding heat's inertia
    as it speeds toward ash

the mystery keeps
    its landscapes rare

presenting a series of photos
    of the same bare place

vacant to the horizon
    the seeing eye thinks

outward from its source
    the way found objects

are lighted from within
    here comes nothing

its old sea-roar
    shapeless in the ear

XXXIX

in China the word
    for picture

consists of two windows
    both completely empty

a perfect transparency
    is nothing at all

concealed by its brightness
    subtle in its grandeur

XL

(After Pascal)

we save and spend god
      the one we created

but god spends nothing
      saves nothing

and soon disappears
      into the number one

god is the proposition
      and its denial

nature and mind
      perfection and disorder

in equal measure
      all wagers are lost

god goes nowhere
      breathes all air

infinity is memory
      when a god plays life

XLI

where is a written deer
running through a written forest
　　　—Wisława Symborska

the written man in bed
　　　with his unwritten wife

she who has written
　　　his figure in that place

experience that lives
　　　only in the written

a dark brown mouse
　　　crossing to the mirror

vacant fishermen
　　　staring into ponds

as if to write them
　　　naked with indifference

what is fire writing
　　　in the house of darkness

all inner space imagined
　　　nothing in shadow

everything that is
　　　written by what is not

XLII

sweat and breath
    the listing of parts

the body of love
    and heat beneath the skin

the rigors of being
    easy in your mind

and in your body hard
    the shape of light

is everywhere at once
    she speaks you into being

draws you from her eyes
    until the threshold enters

and silence grows still

XLIII

rain is falling somewhere
    in this dry world

lightning with its cane
    strides across the field

sometimes thrusting
    itself through the house

the path of darkness
    sweeps everywhere at once

hesitant thunder
    and a change in the air

rain on the river
    making it rush

XLIV

the ones I've offended
    let me kiss your mouths

as poets do endlessly
    between the legs of wells

love is a language
    few of us can speak

if it happens to die
    the mourners are ready

to plunder our grief
    silence make moan

XLV

life imitates art
        when art is at its worst

Christina Aguilera
        and Andy Warhol

grace a page together
        & I must place my eye

beneath the skirts of bells
        nothing lasts forever

except the works of nature
        returning every spring

XLVI

a lovely winter wedding
        for every mother's son

in a world of afternoons
        social observations

mean almost nothing
        Taylor loves John

a mirror loves the sun
        each time I dream

it happens more slowly
        until a fondness comes

XLVII

hollow of the mouth
    velvet of the tongue

the longest intermission
    in the history of song

likeness now begins and
    difference shuts down

how many words
    must grace the poor child

until she feels impassive
    the semblance and the tangle

are models of desire
    little sleep machine

on its way to language
    flickering out of time

XLVIII

jostled by the present
      the future's intermittent

whatever's unfulfilled
      stands at the ready

the way that gives way
      is like a fossil now

when things are unconcealed
      our face to face encounters

are closed to the closed
      we stand among the open

garrulous as they are
      what is not missing

and what was never there
      nothing infinite lasts

the cry of an owl
      is its first world

XLIX

(For Robert Creeley)

never less than present
    and close to the rain

summer's in a rush
    to wet its lips again

something calls us home
    through the dim evening

a pair of hedge clippers
    for those of us who dream

the exhaustions of infinity
    will never touch us now

only gods die and the poor
    love it well

what has always been
    remains to be seen

memory's last station
    too many travelers

The Reading

"I am absent but deep in this absence."
—*Vicente Huidobro*

Someone was
speaking of

"the infinite resources
of the thickness

of things."
I had wanted

so thick
a vessel

it contained
nothing at all.

. . .

For example,
Francis Ponge

touching with
his nouns

the texture
of objects,

as if they
had windows

and desire
were all about.

What are the names
for the opposite of *pencil*,

engineer and *dowel*?
What is not *cloud*,

and what is not *mouse*?
You can't create nothing,

and you can't destroy it.

. . .

Nulla, nulla
the world

keeps weeping,
filling the holes

invention
keeps creating.

Something is complex
and nothing is complex

until culture takes it
or a comet comes crashing,

bearing its dust from
the time of creation.

Tragedy of course
is when a man falls

and his soul
falls with him.

. . .

Something resists experience
and also the sentence,

tendril in the dark
seeking what it finds.

It likes to keep extending
across the range of doubt,

where truth is the unspoken
and beauty's misaligned.

Creation needs its rift
busy with silence,

where the path-hedge waits
to divide us from appearance

& grammar finds its owl.

. . .

All the light in the world
and the light that's missing.

Light coming back
in the eyes of the present.

Small shabby wings
and one of those broken,

its large mouth open
as if to say nothing.

Sense and madness
of course are inherent;

a soul must be acquired
by means of aesthetics,

a life of excess
or a sense of other lives.

. . .

One could always live
in a trailer with pillars

or find employment
as connotative baggage.

I am not well
between hell and heaven

and guilty of a crisis.

What corruption
lies hidden,

enshrouded by
language,

what substance,
what bride,

temptations of
the infinite

in what
corrosive tongue?

. . .

A way of emerging
from our pastel lives

into the carnal
glare of language,

where desire has
words with itself

and the nude
fact stands.

At the angle
of shining

on a frozen
winter day—

flat fields,
thin lake—

a window's
the only color,

something like
a soul.

. . .

The flurry skimming
toward you

over pale ground
the way light writes

vaguely over a surface.

As when
in the fall

a leaf
gives heat

and a final
word is spoken

by someone
who forgets

in the middle
of his sentence

what it is
to speak.

. . .

The solidity
of the fragment,

divisible
by nothing,

gloomy in
its grandeur.

Lake bed quiet,
covered with snow,

no sound whatever
even on the roads.

Hearts underground
make their history

only in this—
seed pod moving,

shaken by wind

. . .

When the carpenter
hits the nail,

seconds of silence
and then

a long sound
distorted by

its journey.

A small harmonica
broken from its key chain

remains in his pocket.
He can't play a note

but then at a party
plays six bars

and it seems authentic
because he stops.

. . .

Mirrors in the cat
and noises

known to dogs,
the utter realism

of standing
face to face

and that
also fictive.

Altogether simple,
the mystery

of the figure,
its face unhinged

by experience
and the angle.

So which
do you prefer,

the "continuous present,"
or a realistic

fiction with its
authentic now?

. . .

Not Madonna kissing your face
not even monks at swordplay

but the raw inaction
of a hero who wants nothing,

plastic hands at his mouth,
pink light through his arms.

The spaces
between things

assume their own shapes
as vacancies on call—

darkness between
two towns,

lights within
the lights,

a solemn feast
of attention

and tedium
standing firm.

. . .

Where the boats
rock at odds,

a song of
the dimensions.

Alarming appetite
for living in history,

confined by our pleasures,
always on call.

.   .   .

If I understand
your meaning,

it's perfectly OK
to manipulate

distance by
standing near it.

You can smudge
the real and

have it come
to feeling.

I like it,
she said,

the way I
understand it.

. . .

Cliché of
the potato

and also
of the wing.

Never to say
confusedly

in the company
of others

or inhabit
other things

except with
your mind.

A lot of loose talk
was going around town

about an "infinity of truths,"
and the sheriff was missing.

I had to ponder alone
the color of corn

and the infinite object
I'd come to know so well.

. . .

Beware the good man.
He has no forgiveness.

Half of him remains
a permanent condition.

The other half remembers
horizons like constructions.

the moth begat the flame
thought begat sand

light begat the hand
the hand begat its name

the eyes begat shape
shape begat a cage

spine begat lamp
lamp begat the page

. . .

Something written and
something erased.

Archeology of the paint
seven layers down.

The generations stripped
down to their words.

These familiar things
are trying us on for size.

To carry awareness
around all day

as if fond of desolation,
a raw landscape

stripped of its feelings,
frenzy for the eyes.

. . . .

Two black spaniels
are all I
think I know

and not one
typical except in
its distress at

a future by
the sea, salt
wind blowing

between the
crabbing nets and
beach blue sky.

Touch is elusive
but it makes
you feel at home

in the body
you'd been seeking.

. . .

Perhaps inaction painting
is what we're looking for—

silence between the lines,
color between words.

Tender mercies of sound
because shapes feel

and the turning mind turns.
Accuracies of a map

held up backwards,
the roads shining through.

Meatier so to speak,
a thick impasto

of history without
its thinking,

science exhausted
by the cruelty of paint.

. . .

Or something innate happens,
slapped onto the canvas

with classical restrictions
we'd forgotten the edges of.

Rain on gray slate.
Reticence of the city.

. . .

Within the linear forest,
at the edge of all scatter,

beyond recognition
but coming into focus,

where color folds and
dust resists the garden,

a fruit tree stands—
dots and dashes.

OTHER POETRY TITLES FROM APOGEE PRESS

Maxine Chernoff
Among the Names

Valerie Coulton
passing world pictures

Tsering Wangmo Dhompa
In the Absent Everyday
Rules of the House

Kathleen Fraser
Discrete Categories Forced into Coupling

Alice Jones
Gorgeous Mourning

Stefanie Marlis
cloudlife
fine

Edward Kleinschmidt Mayes
Speed of Life

Pattie McCarthy
bk of (h)rs
Verso

Denise Newman
Human Forest

Elizabeth Robinson
Apostrophe
Apprehend

Edward Smallfield
The Pleasures of C

Cole Swensen
Oh

Truong Tran
dust and conscience
placing the accents
within the margin

TO ORDER OR FOR MORE INFORMATION GO TO
WWW.APOGEEPRESS.COM

PAUL HOOVER'S poetry books include *Poems in Spanish*, which was nominated for the Bay Area Book Award, *Winter (Mirror)*, *Rehearsal in Black*, and *Totem and Shadow: New and Selected Poems*. He is editor of the anthology *Postmodern American Poetry* (W. W. Norton) and co-editor of the influential literary magazine, *New American Writing*. With Maxine Chernoff, he has translated *Selected Poems of Friedrich Hölderlin* and, with Nguyen Do, *Contemporary Vietnamese Poetry*. Professor of Creative Writing at San Francisco State University, he has also published a collection of literary essays, *Fables of Representation*.